SIMULATING WEATHER EXPERIMENTS FOR KIDS

SCIENCE BOOK OF EXPERIMENTS

CHILDREN'S SCIENCE EDUCATION BOOKS

BABY PROFESSOR

EDUCATION KIDS

Speedy Publishing LLC

40 E. Main St. #1156

Newark, DE 19711

www.speedypublishing.com

Copyright 2017

tue	wed	thu	fri	sat	sun
12°	17°	20°	15°	14°	10°

In this book, we're going to talk about the weather and some simple experiments you can do at home or school. Make sure an adult is there to help you so you're safe when conducting experiments. So, let's get right to it!

HOW DOES RAIN FORM?

Water is always on the move. Water that fell in rain on your house yesterday may have been part of an ocean wave a few days before.

RAIN FLOWS DOWN FROM A ROOF

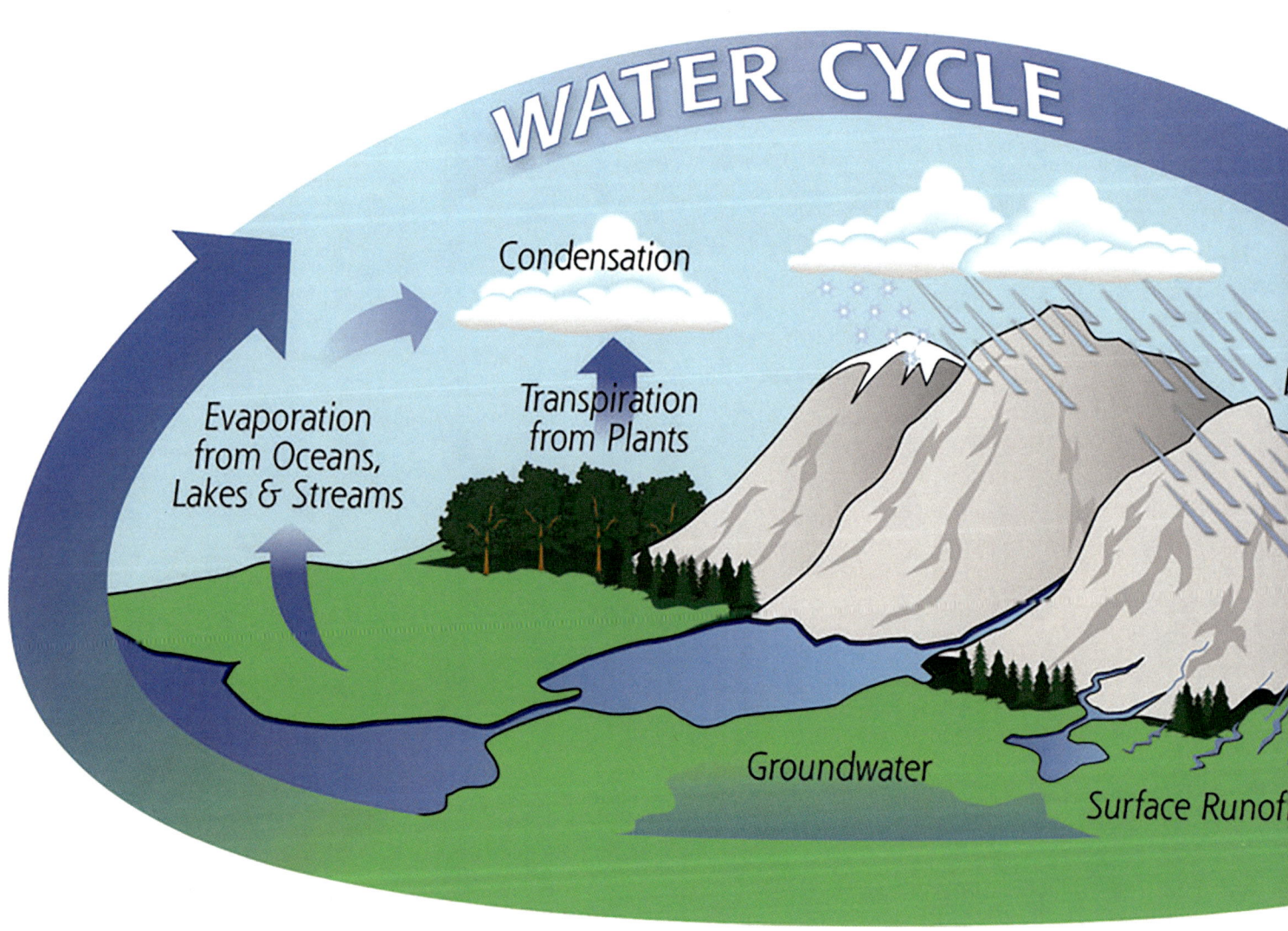

WATER CYCLE

Condensation

Evaporation
from Oceans,
Lakes & Streams

Transpiration
from Plants

Groundwater

Surface Runoff

...tion

Although you can't see it, there's quite a bit of water in the air. There's also water on the surface of the land, in all Earth's waterways, and underground. The water changes form and then gets used repeatedly in a process described as the water cycle. Water goes from its liquid form to ice, which is a solid, to water vapor, which is a gas.

As the sun beats down, the water at the top surfaces of waterways evaporates into the atmosphere. The water vapor goes up into the atmosphere, and as it cools, it creates tiny water droplets. This process of cooling is called condensation. These droplets create what we see as clouds in the air.

WATER DROPLETS ON A LEAF

FIELD BEFORE THE BIG STORM

As the droplets combine, they start to get bigger and bigger until they're too heavy to stay in the atmosphere. That's when we get a big rainstorm and the rain falls down on the ground and the cycle starts all over again.

Rain isn't the only thing that falls from clouds. Depending on the weather conditions, hail or snow can fall too.

EXPERIMENT 1

WATER CYCLE IN A BOWL

To do this experiment, you'll need a large clear bowl, a small plastic cup, plastic wrap, water, a coin to use as a weight, and a sunny location outdoors.

BOWL

PLASTIC CUP

Place the small plastic cup in the center of your bowl. Fill the bowl with water, but make sure you don't fill it so much that water gets into the plastic cup. You don't want any water in the plastic cup when you set up the experiment.

Cover the top of the bowl with plastic wrap and make sure it's secure around the edges. Then, place a coin over the plastic wrap located over the plastic cup. You just want to make sure the plastic wrap is pushed down on top of the plastic cup.

Put the bowl of water in a sunny location and leave it there for a few days. The sun's heat will make the water evaporate.

PLASTIC WRAP

COINS

The water will rise and form condensation on the cool surface of the plastic wrap. Then, the water will fall back down into the small container. The water that has fallen in the small container is the rain portion of the water cycle. You've created a mini version of the water cycle in a bowl!

EXPLANATION: The water in your bowl is like the water in a large lake. The heat from the sun has made the water evaporate and it goes into the atmosphere. Then, it condenses and falls back down again, into the empty plastic cup. Your plastic cup had its own rainfall.

SUNLIGHT SHOWING EVAPORATION FROM SEA

SNOWFLAKES

EXPERIMENT 2

STUDYING SNOWFLAKES

To do this experiment, you'll need a piece of black fabric, a good quality magnifying glass, and snowy weather.

Put the black fabric into your freezer for about two hours. Now, take it outdoors when it's snowing. Wait until some snowflakes fall on top of the fabric.

Look at the snowflakes with your magnifying glass to see their unique six-sided shapes. No two snowflakes are exactly the same. Isn't that amazing?

BLACK FABRIC

A GIRL HOLDING EMPTY PLASTIC BOTTLES

EXPERIMENT 3

MAKING YOUR OWN CLOUD

To do this experiment, you'll need a 2-liter clear plastic soda bottle, matches, and some warm water.

Make sure to remove the label from your bottle and wash it out so it's completely clear. Pour about 2 centimeters of very hot water, about 130 degrees Fahrenheit, into the bottom of the bottle. Don't use boiling water though, because it may warp the plastic. Swirl the water through the bottle to warm up the inside a little.

Have an adult help you with this next part. Strike one match and then blow it completely out after 3-4 seconds. While it's still smoking, put it inside the head of the bottle so the smoke goes in. The smoke will disappear. Throw the match away and quickly screw the top on the bottle. Make sure not to squeeze the sides of the bottle while you do this. You don't want any of the smoke to escape.

Squeeze the bottle's sides hard at least three times. Then, wait a few seconds, and squeeze it again. This time hold it longer before releasing it.

You should have created your own tiny cloud in a bottle!

SQUEEZING THE BOTTLE

CLOUDS

EXPLANATION: This experiment is a snapshot of what happens when clouds are created in the sky. When you press in on the bottle's sides, you're actually compressing the molecules of water. When you release the sides, the air inside expands, and as a result, the temperature decreases. As the air continues to cool, the molecules can stick to each other more quickly. They form clumps of droplets that are attached to the smoke in your bottle's atmosphere.

EXPERIMENT 4

MAKE YOUR OWN THUNDERSTORM

To do this experiment, you'll need a large flat, plastic container about the same size and depth as a shoebox. You'll need to make some ice cubes ahead of time with blue food coloring in them. You'll also need red food coloring.

ICE CUBES

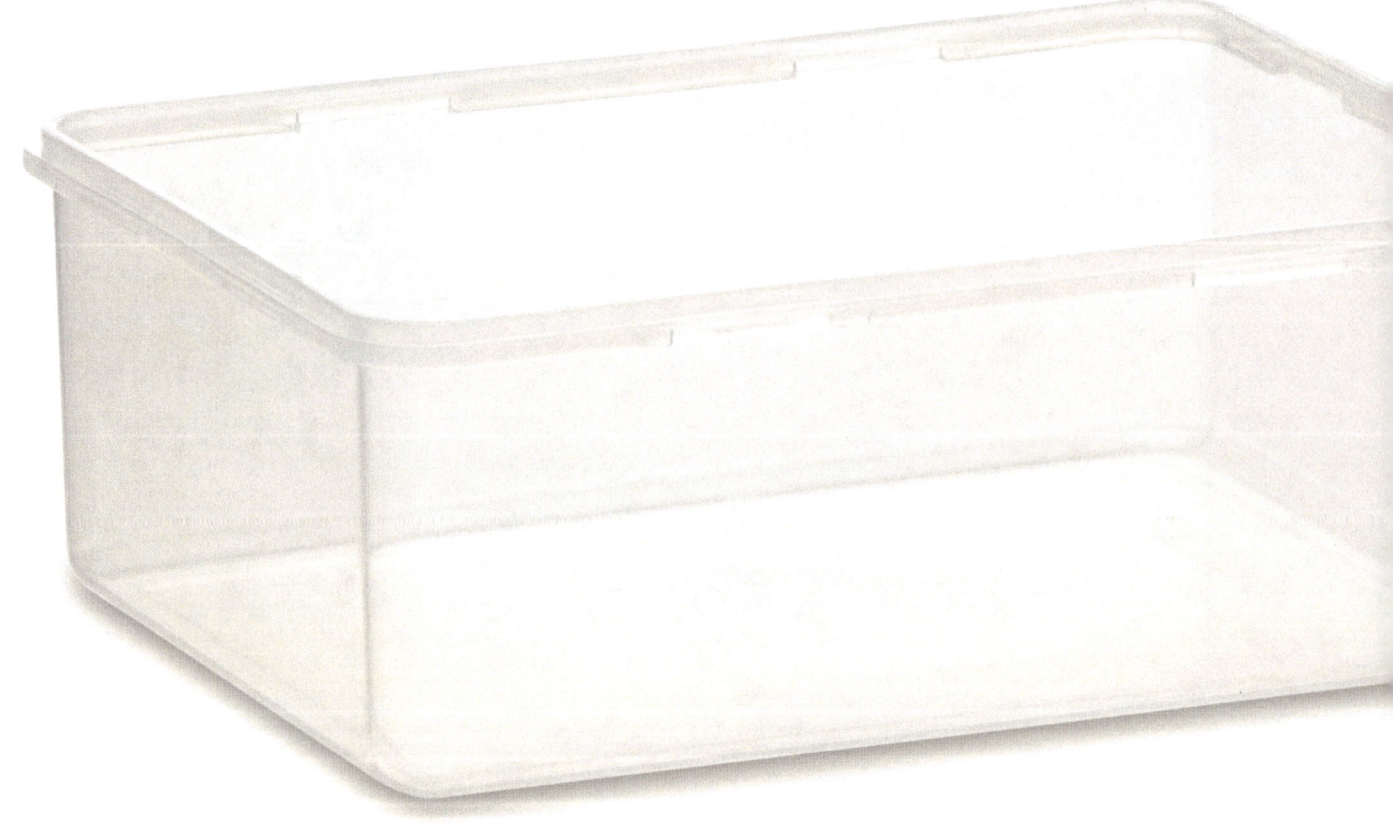

Fill the plastic container up with warm water from your tap. Wait one minute before starting. Then, place two blue ice cubes at one end of the container. Place the red food coloring, about three drops, in the water at the other end of the container.

As the blue ice melts, you will see that it goes to the water in the bottom of the container. The warm water and red food coloring will go up to the top of the container.

EXPLANATION: This experiment uses water instead of air to show the process of convection. The hot water rises just like the hot air in a thunderstorm. The blue water and ice represent the approaching cold front. When unstable warm air is pushed into higher altitudes by a moving cold front, thunderstorms are formed.

FOOD COLORING

CUTE BOY WITH COLORFUL BALLOONS

EXPERIMENT 5

MAKE A MODEL OF LIGHTNING

To do this experiment, you'll need a blown-up rubber balloon, a fluorescent light bulb, and a dark room.

Blow up the balloon and tie it up so the air doesn't escape. Turn the lights off in the room. Rub the balloon on top of your head for 5-10 seconds. Now hold the balloon, which has static electricity, close to the bottom of the light bulb. It should light up!

GIRL WITH STATIC HAIR

EXPLANATION: By rubbing the balloon on your hair and head, you built up a type of electrical charge called static electricity. When you touch the balloon to the bottom of the bulb, the electricity jumps from the balloon and turns on the light inside the bulb.

As the hot and cold air in the atmosphere create a thunderstorm, the clouds become filled with electrical charges. When the electricity increases to a certain level, it becomes powerful enough to jump across from one location to another. A lightning spark can be generated from a cloud or it can jump from one cloud to a second cloud.

THUNDERSTORM WITH RAIN AND LIGHTNING BOLTS

ORLANDO, FLORIDA SKYLINE

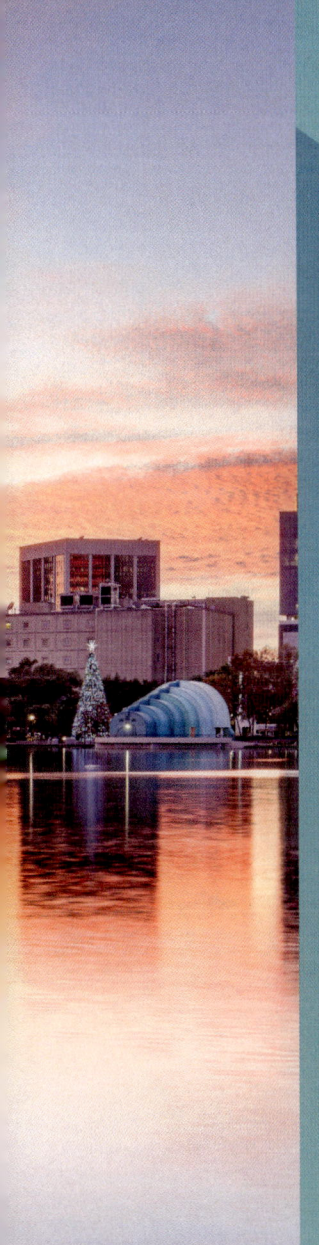

It can also go from a cloud to the ground or the opposite way from the ground up to a cloud.

Lightning strikes the ground on Earth about 8 million times every day! Most of the strikes from the clouds to the ground in the United States occur on the land between Orlando and Tampa in Florida where there is a lot of moisture in the atmosphere.

WHAT IS A TORNADO?

Tornadoes are rotating cones of air that come from a thunderstorm down to the ground or water. Most tornadoes are very dangerous. They can reach speeds over 300 miles per hour and they destroy everything in their path as they move along the ground. In the United States, over 1,000 tornadoes are reported every year.

TORNADO AFTERMATH

EXPERIMENT 6

MAKE YOUR OWN TORNADO

To do this experiment, you'll need a clear plastic or glass mayonnaise or mason jar, some clear liquid soap like dishwashing liquid, white vinegar, and water. You'll also need food coloring and glitter.

Fill your jar up to about three-fourths of its capacity with water. Add one teaspoon of dishwashing liquid and a teaspoon of white vinegar. Add in a few drops of food coloring and a teaspoon or two of glitter.

Shake up the jar and then twirl it in a circle. The liquid inside will form a tiny tornado. Luckily, this tornado can't cause any destruction except for some clean-up!

GLITTER

TORNADO

EXPLANATION: The motion you did by twirling the jar gives the liquid a vortex. It models the action of a thunderstorm during a tornado.

WEATHER:

Awesome! Now you know more about the weather by doing your own experiments. You can find more Science Education books from Baby Professor by searching the website of your favorite book retailer.

Visit

BABY PROFESSOR
EDUCATION KIDS

www.BabyProfessorBooks.com

to download Free Baby Professor eBooks and view
our catalog of new and exciting Children's Books

Made in the USA
Middletown, DE
03 December 2020